Costume in Context

Underwear

c. 1991

c. 1901

Jennifer Ruby

B T Batsford Ltd, London

Foreword

The idea behind the *Costume in Context* and *People in Costume* (for younger children) series is to show clothes worn throughout the ages by people from all walks of life.

This volume on underwear is slightly different in that it examines the underwear worn beneath fashionable garments and, of course, until recent times, only the wealthy could afford to be fashionable. Poor people had to be much more practical and would not have been able to work had they been wearing some of the more unusual structures illustrated in this book.

Many of the characters from *Costume in Context* reappear here and you will learn about some of the tortures they endured in order to present a fine outward appearance. The 'Interesting Facts' page might encourage you to find out more facts and anecdotes for yourself and the 'Things to Do' section contains ideas for projects and follow-up work.

Acknowledgements

The sources for the drawings have, in many cases, been contemporary prints and pictures. I would like to acknowledge the following:

Colour plates: (3) left hand figure after Allan Ramsay; (5) advert for Bon Ton and Royal Worcester Kidfitting Corsets c. 1913; (6) La Vie Parisienne c. 1930; (7) after fashion drawings by Isao Yajima; page 7 after Rowlandson; page 23 after John Collet; page 44 Arrow advertisement 1935

This book is for Trevor, who rescued me and gave me back my life.

c. 1923

© Jennifer Ruby 1996
First published 1996

Printed in the UK by The Bath Press
for the publishers
B.T. Batsford Ltd
4 Fitzhardinge Street
London W1H 0AH

A CIP catalogue record for this book is available from the British Library.

ISBN 0 7134 7663 X

Contents

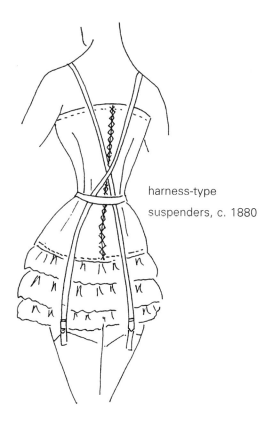

harness-type suspenders, c. 1880

Interesting Facts

In medieval times, religious attitudes taught that the body was sinful and that underwear, being next to the body, was therefore something shameful. This is why we read of penance being conducted in shirts and smocks and pilgrims wearing hair shirts.

During the second half of the sixteenth century, the rigid look of women's fashions was partly achieved by wearing a busk in the centre front of the corset. These garments were so constricting and painful that they could cause miscarriages.

In 1564 starch was introduced into England by a Dutch woman who gave expensive lessons on how to starch to wealthy ladies. As knowledge of starching gradually became more widespread, the fashionable neck ruff got larger and larger.

The lace collar supported on a frame which was fashionable at the beginning of the seventeenth century could cost the equivalent of a year's wages for a working man (£3-£4). Obviously, it was only worn by the very rich.

The first publicity slogan for underwear appeared in the window of a corset maker in the seventeenth century. The controlling effects of the corset were advertised thus: 'It controls the large, supports the small, uplifts the drooping'!

In the eighteenth century the corset was already being criticised on the grounds that tight lacing was harmful to health. However, women were also advised to beware of the 'immorality' of loose garments which hid the shape of the body: loose garments were usually associated with a 'loose' woman.

During the eighteenth and nineteenth centuries hooped petticoats caused numerous accidents. Perhaps one of the worst was in 1863 when 2000 women were burnt to death in the cathedral of Santiago when their flimsy dresses worn over crinolines were ignited by candles.

In 1876 French dancers caused great excitement at Leicester Square in London because they were wearing suspenders to keep up their stockings. By 1878 many British women were wearing suspenders. The first type were fixed on a harness that went over the shoulders.

During the 1870s, curvature of the spine caused by tight lacing was diagnosed as frequently as a slipped disc is today. The desire to alter the natural body shape is still strong. Modern man goes to the gym to alter his physique and then adorns it with figure-hugging lycra: he could be said to be wearing an invisible corset of diet and exercise!

Can you find out some more interesting facts?

Introduction

The subject of underwear is a fascinating one. Perhaps this is partly because underwear has so many different functions but it is also because it is usually hidden from view and so its mystery arouses interest.

Its first function is protection. Underwear protects the body from cold and provides some degree of modesty for the wearer. In centuries past, it also protected outergarments. Personal cleanliness was not thought to be important until towards the close of the eighteenth century, so the magnificent and costly fabrics used for costumes before this time needed to be kept away from the filthy skin of the person wearing them!

Throughout history men and women have strived to alter their physical shape in order to achieve a fashionable silhouette. This might be done either by paring down the body or adding on to it. Paring down could be agony and might be achieved by bandaging, tight lacing or boned corsets. People have often carried this to such extremes that it has been damaging to their health. For example, in 1814 the Prince Regent was told by his anxious doctors that he must stop squeezing his portly figure into tight stays as they were endangering his life! Adding on to the body involves ingenious padding and mysterious appliances worn in strategic places. These have often been known to slip out of place, causing considerable embarrassment to the person concerned.

Underwear also supports the shape of costume and, as outlines change with the fashions, so too do the undergarments beneath. In fact, some of the fantastically exaggerated shapes of clothes from the past can only be understood by looking at the unusual underwear beneath.

For centuries social classes could be differentiated by the underwear that they wore. For example, the frills and lace on the shirt of a seventeenth-century gentleman would clearly distinguish him from the manual worker who would be wearing a plain practical garment. In addition, the more complicated and restricting the underwear, the more likely it would be that the wearer would belong to the leisured rather than the working class. Materials were significant too; fine linen being preferable to coarse cotton and wool, and only the very rich being able to afford silk.

Finally, underwear is used to attract the opposite sex. To reveal portions of underclothes can be seen as a provocative act and symbolizes the act of undressing. In our day, after mini skirts and hot pants, it is hard for us to imagine how easy it would be for an eighteenth-century woman to make her lover blush merely by revealing her petticoat! The body's centre of attraction tends to go in and out of fashion and whether bosoms, bottoms or legs are the current focus affects the corresponding items of underwear used to enhance that particular part of the anatomy.

Another interesting phenomenon is the way in which outergarments have become undergarments and vice versa. For example, the early Saxon breeches shrank and eventually became drawers and the tightly-laced

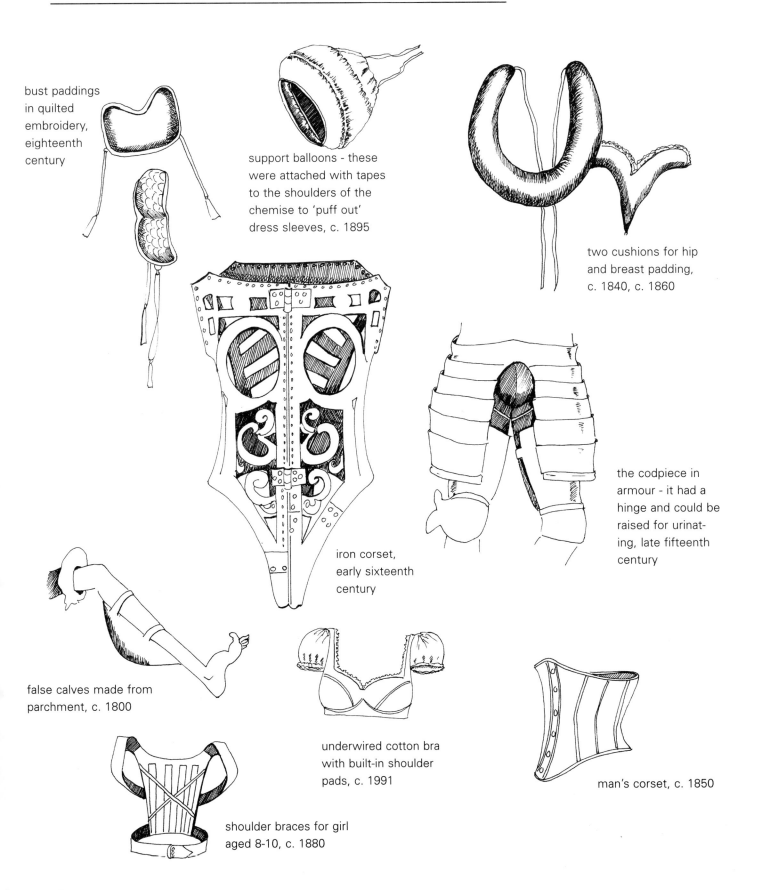

bust paddings in quilted embroidery, eighteenth century

support balloons - these were attached with tapes to the shoulders of the chemise to 'puff out' dress sleeves, c. 1895

two cushions for hip and breast padding, c. 1840, c. 1860

iron corset, early sixteenth century

the codpiece in armour - it had a hinge and could be raised for urinating, late fifteenth century

false calves made from parchment, c. 1800

underwired cotton bra with built-in shoulder pads, c. 1991

man's corset, c. 1850

shoulder braces for girl aged 8-10, c. 1880

bodices of medieval gowns became the corsets of later years. Conversely, men's shirts, at one time considered to be underwear, have now risen to the surface and the same is true of women's stockings which in the past were rarely revealed.

In this book you will meet some of the characters who appeared in the *Costume in Context* series. You will see them in their underwear and often in the outerwear which goes on top. Perhaps you could reflect on some of the points mentioned above while you are reading and this will help to deepen your understanding of the history of costume.

1791

Early Medieval, 1066-1300

In medieval times, underwear was relatively simple. Next to their skin, men wore a loose shirt which was made of wool, linen or, for the wealthy, silk. In addition to this men wore braies. These were a loose, trouser-like garment made of linen. At first braies were in effect an outergarment, but as fashions changed and more layers were added on top they became an undergarment. As time wore on they gradually became shorter and tighter, as shown in the picture below.

John is a Norman and a rich landowner. He is wearing a fine linen shirt with side vents and braies which have been cross-gartered with linen strips below the knees.

c. 1070

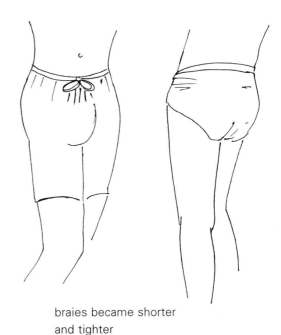

braies became shorter
and tighter

The only undergarment known to be worn by women at this time was the smock, later called the chemise. It was slipped on over the head and worn next to the skin.

John's wife is pictured here in her chemise which is made from chainsil, a silk material. On top of this she will wear her gown and a girdle.

As time progressed and the outergown became more fitted, it is probable that the chemise underwent a similar change in style though there is no firm evidence to support this.

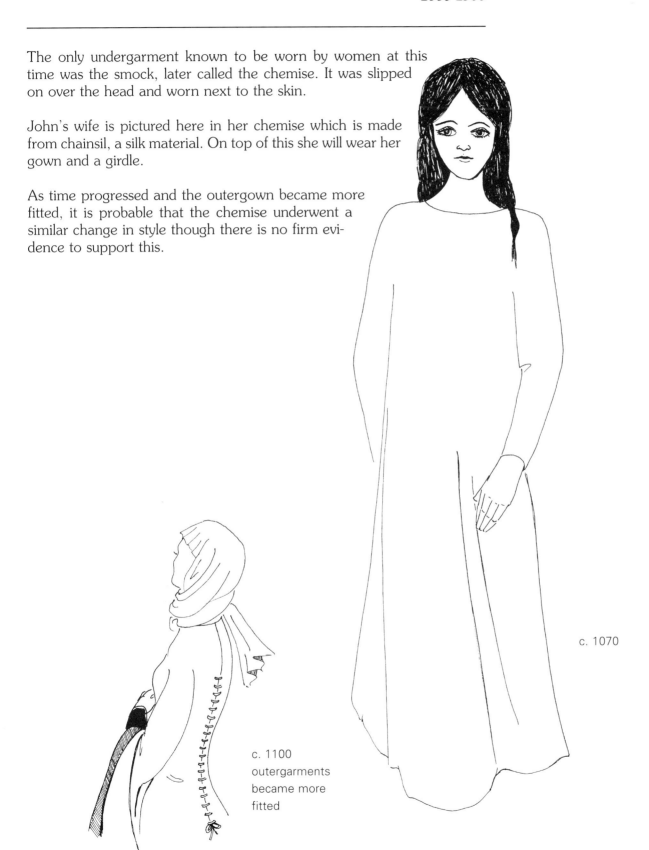

c. 1070

c. 1100
outergarments
became more
fitted

Late Medieval, 1300-1485

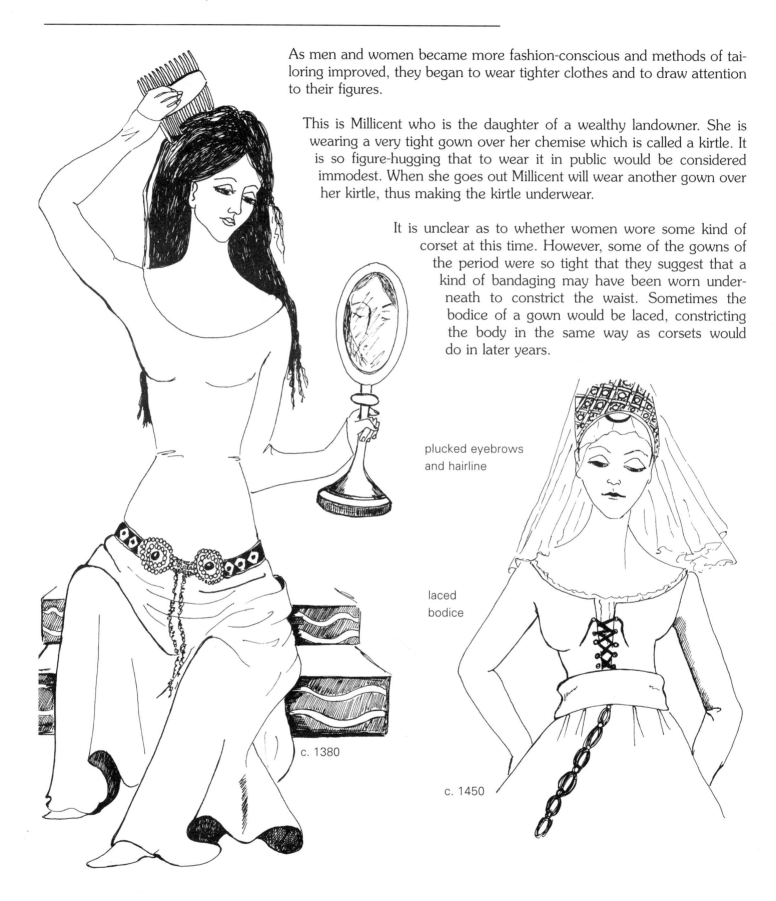

As men and women became more fashion-conscious and methods of tailoring improved, they began to wear tighter clothes and to draw attention to their figures.

This is Millicent who is the daughter of a wealthy landowner. She is wearing a very tight gown over her chemise which is called a kirtle. It is so figure-hugging that to wear it in public would be considered immodest. When she goes out Millicent will wear another gown over her kirtle, thus making the kirtle underwear.

It is unclear as to whether women wore some kind of corset at this time. However, some of the gowns of the period were so tight that they suggest that a kind of bandaging may have been worn underneath to constrict the waist. Sometimes the bodice of a gown would be laced, constricting the body in the same way as corsets would do in later years.

plucked eyebrows and hairline

laced bodice

c. 1380

c. 1450

As men began to wear hose (stockings), braies eventually became so short they were little more than a loin cloth tied around the waist. At first, hose had separate legs and were kept up by being fastened to the doublet (jacket) by means of laces which were called points. However, as outergarments became shorter, the legs were united forming a garment like our modern tights. The codpiece, fashionable from 1408-1575, was a small pouch worn over the genitals. It was fastened together with points.

Thomas is a squire and is training to be a knight. He is wearing a fashionably short doublet and hose. The doublet sleeves are gathered at the shoulder over mahoitres (shoulder pads).

eyelet
holes

shirt

loin cloth
tied at the
waist

points

hose

tights with
codpiece

c. 1460

Early Tudor, 1485-1550

During the first part of the sixteenth century, women's fashions were very simple and had soft flowing lines. As time wore on, more rigid and artificial structures were used to create a different silhouette.

This is Cecily who lives with her husband and their family on their large estate in the Midlands. She is wearing a gown with a stiffened bodice which flattens her chest. Her chemise is visible at the neckline and wrists of her gown and also on her sleeves where it has been pulled through slashes (cuts) in the material. Sometimes Cecily wears a stiffened bodice under her gown like the one pictured below.

It was at this time that women first began to wear petticoats. These were tied on around the waist.

c. 1530

a bodice stiffened with whalebone or steel

When Henry VIII was on the throne men's fashions were square-shaped and aggressively masculine. They seemed to echo the power and strength of the proud male monarch.

This is Cecily's husband, Richard. He is wearing a gown with excessively padded shoulders which gives him a square silhouette. His codpiece, another symbol of masculinity, is large and highly decorated. Sometimes he uses it to keep money in! His shirt is exquisitely embroidered and has a high neckline. This neckline will eventually develop into the ruff that will be fashionable later in the century. Hose are now divided into two parts, upper and lower, sometimes called upper stocks and nether stocks. The upper hose are often made from a different material to the lower hose, as in Richard's outft. Gradually upper hose were to become more bulbous in shape and were padded with cotton, wool or horsehair. This padding was called bombast.

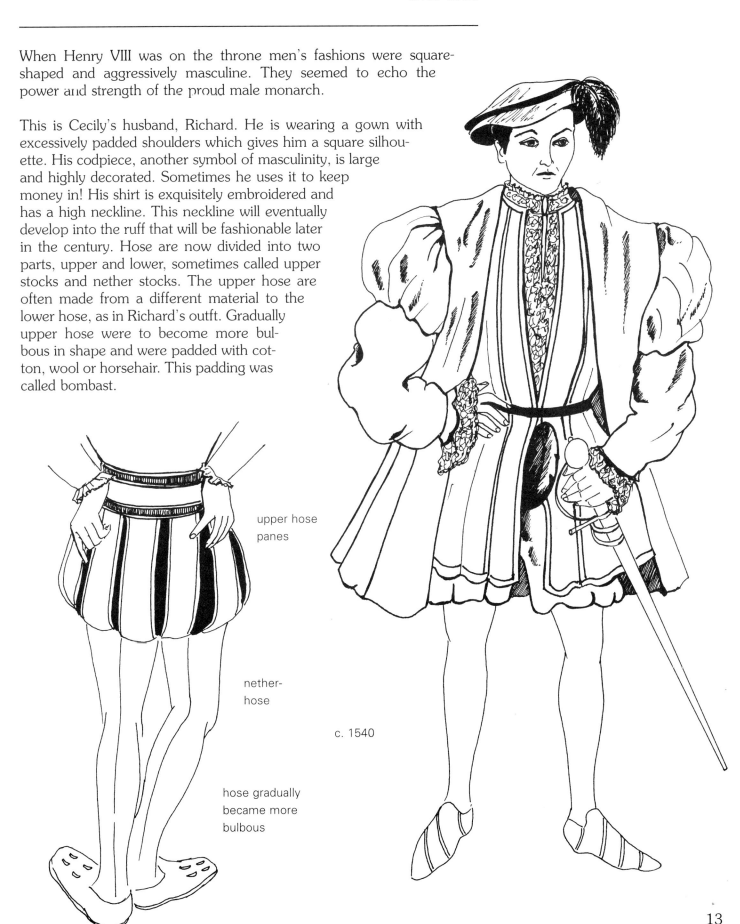

upper hose
panes

nether-
hose

c. 1540

hose gradually
became more
bulbous

Late Tudor, 1550 -1603

This is Nicholas who lives and works at court where he is a firm favourite with Queen Elizabeth I.

Men's fashions have changed quite drastically and it is interesting that they have a more effeminate look now that there is a woman on the throne.

Nicholas is wearing a starched ruff and also has ruffs at his wrists. His upper hose, or trunk hose, are very padded, emphasizing his hips, and his codpiece is large and decorative. His trunk hose are attached to his lower hose with points.

Nicholas's doublet has a peascod belly. This strange fashion involves padding the front of the belly so that it overhangs the waist like a paunch. The padding is a pointed shape and some of Nicholas's friends have it as long as 24cm so it is almost impossible for them to bend over!

c. 1577

points

points to attach upper
hose to lower hose

Nicholas's sister Catherine is a lady-in-waiting at the court. You can see how rigid and uncomfortable women's fashions have become.

Like her brother, Catherine is wearing a large ruff at her neck and has smaller ruffs at her wrists. Her gown has a 'V' opening which is filled in with a stomacher, the material of which matches the inverted 'V' opening of the skirt. Her chemise is visible above the stomacher and below the ruff.

Under her skirt Catherine is wearing a Spanish farthingale. This is an underpetticoat with a series of hoops, smaller at the top, inserted into it at intervals. It is similar to the crinoline that will be popular in Queen Victoria's reign. The farthingale gives Catherine's skirt a bell-like shape.

c. 1580

Spanish farthingale

embroidered stomacher

Cartwheels and Bum-rolls, 1570-1625

In about 1570 the French farthingale appeared and began to compete with the Spanish version. The Spanish farthingale was worn by all classes but the French farthingale was more exclusive. Both remained on the fashion scene until about 1625.

The French farthingale looked like a horizontal cartwheel with a tub-shaped hooped petticoat beneath. The wheel part tilted forward slightly in order to accommodate the elongated front of the stiffened bodice. Petticoats and skirts were then draped over the top.

The bum-roll was an alternative for those women who could not afford such extravagant and cumbersome fashions. It was a thick, sausage-shaped bustle which was worn around the waist under the skirt to hold it out.

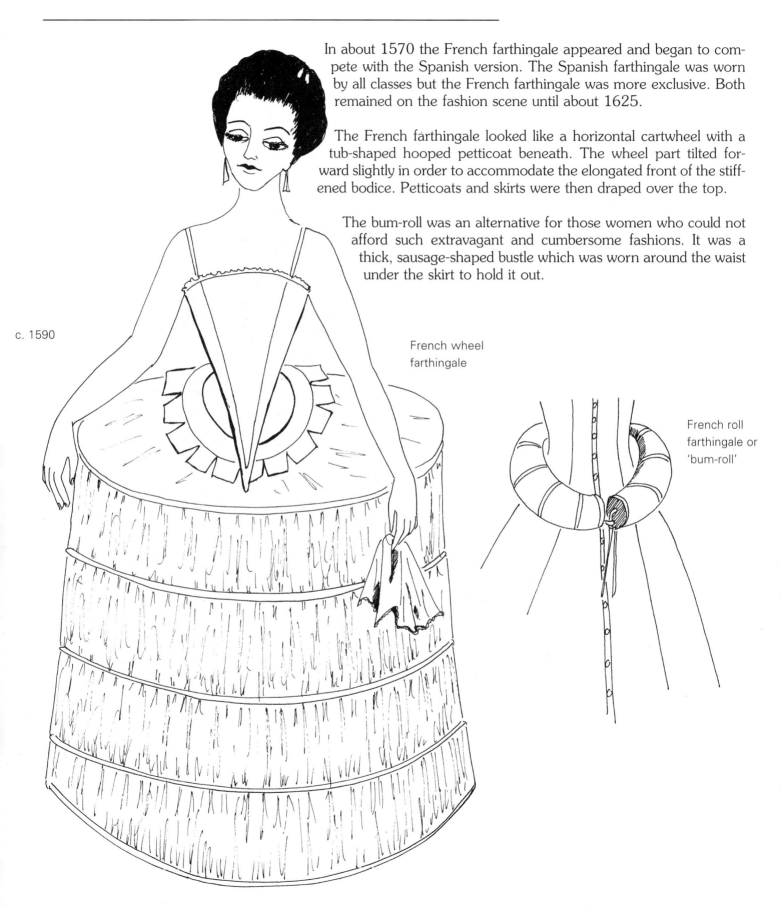

c. 1590

French wheel farthingale

French roll farthingale or 'bum-roll'

On the left you can see Catherine in a French farthingale and on the right is her sister Mary who is wearing a dress over a farthingale petticoat.

This fashion was not only uncomfortable, it was also inconvenient because ladies took up too much space. James I hated farthingales and tried twice to ban them. On one occasion there was an accident when a group of women became wedged in the entrance to a masquing hall!

dress worn over
farthingale, c. 1613

A Cavalier, c. 1635

drawers visible here

Sir Robert is a rich nobleman and a Cavalier. This means that he is a supporter of Charles I in the dispute between the king and Parliament.

From Sir Robert's outfit you can see that a man's silhouette has changed drastically. Instead of lots of padding there is now a much slimmer line.

Underwear is now used much more to attract the opposite sex and reflects social class. It is fashionable to go 'unbuttoned' both in summer and winter, so displaying one's costly shirt at various strategic places. Sir Robert's shirt is showing through the slashes in his doublet and also where his buttons have been left unfastened. The extravagant lace on his shirt collar and cuffs is the mark of a fine gentleman.

What were trunk hose have now developed into breeches. These are attached to the doublet with points and reach to just below the knee. Sir Robert is also wearing white silk stockings and ribbon garters.

Sir Robert has two kinds of drawers. Sometimes he wears short ones, rather like modern trunks, and sometimes long ones which have stirrups under the insteps to stop them slipping up his legs. In the picture you will notice that he has carefully (though supposedly carelessly) left a few of his breeches buttons undone to reveal his drawers at the knee.

silk drawers fastened with ribbons in the front

white linen shirt with very full sleeves; collar and cuffs trimmed with lace; embroidery on shoulders

white linen nightshirt embroidered with silver, gold, red and green

fawn linen stockings with laces for a closer fit

hand knitted boot hose - the wide tops would be folded down over the boots

A Fashionable Lady, 1651

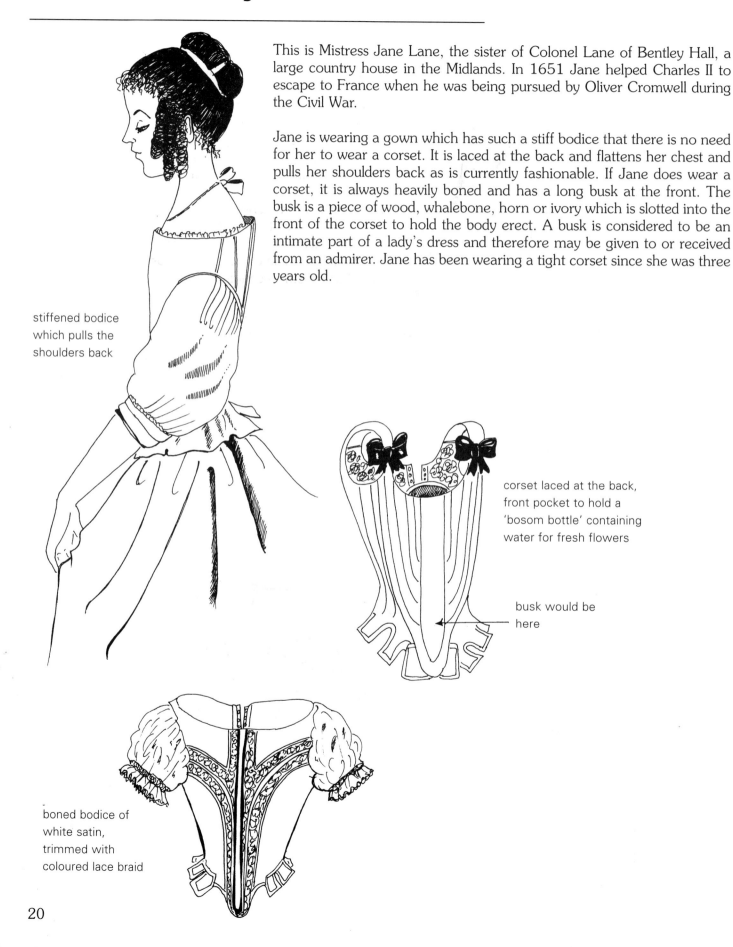

This is Mistress Jane Lane, the sister of Colonel Lane of Bentley Hall, a large country house in the Midlands. In 1651 Jane helped Charles II to escape to France when he was being pursued by Oliver Cromwell during the Civil War.

Jane is wearing a gown which has such a stiff bodice that there is no need for her to wear a corset. It is laced at the back and flattens her chest and pulls her shoulders back as is currently fashionable. If Jane does wear a corset, it is always heavily boned and has a long busk at the front. The busk is a piece of wood, whalebone, horn or ivory which is slotted into the front of the corset to hold the body erect. A busk is considered to be an intimate part of a lady's dress and therefore may be given to or received from an admirer. Jane has been wearing a tight corset since she was three years old.

stiffened bodice which pulls the shoulders back

corset laced at the back, front pocket to hold a 'bosom bottle' containing water for fresh flowers

busk would be here

boned bodice of white satin, trimmed with coloured lace braid

Jane always wears a lace-edged chemise under her corsets and petticoats. As the farthingale is no longer fashionable, she wears at least three petticoats to hold out her skirts. Ladies named these petticoats 'the modest one', 'the mischievous one' and ' the secret one'! Her stockings reach to just over the knee and are often brightly coloured. They are held up with garters that are tied or buckled. Jane never wears drawers as these are considered immodest. At night she wears a lace-edged nightcap and nightdress.

It is worth remembering that men and women were usually dirty at this time as little attention was paid to personal cleanliness. Jane's garments are heavily perfumed and she often wears a posy of fresh flowers at her bosom to counteract any unpleasant odours!

chemise made from holland with a drawstring neck and edged with lace

hand-knitted green silk stocking

nightcap and nightdress edged with lace

A Mill Owner's Wife, c. 1775

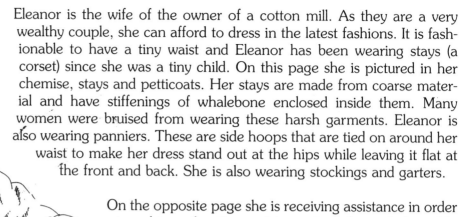

Eleanor is the wife of the owner of a cotton mill. As they are a very wealthy couple, she can afford to dress in the latest fashions. It is fashionable to have a tiny waist and Eleanor has been wearing stays (a corset) since she was a tiny child. On this page she is pictured in her chemise, stays and petticoats. Her stays are made from coarse material and have stiffenings of whalebone enclosed inside them. Many women were bruised from wearing these harsh garments. Eleanor is also wearing panniers. These are side hoops that are tied on around her waist to make her dress stand out at the hips while leaving it flat at the front and back. She is also wearing stockings and garters.

On the opposite page she is receiving assistance in order to achieve the tiny waist required for a fashionable look! In this picture she is wearing pockets which are tied on around her waist.

The corset was very important to women in the eighteenth century as it not only supplied a fashionable shape but also provided warmth. Many women kept their corsets on in bed and even in childbirth. Being tightly laced had another significance in that a laced up woman was believed to be a respectable one, whereas loose stays were thought indicative of loose morals.

a stay busk made from sycamore

When This You See ‡ Pray Think on Me ‡ Tho many Miles We Distant Be ‡

white satin garter

white satin padded with cotton wool

fine wire springs covered with white silk

ribbon tie

A Visit to the Bum Shop, c. 1785

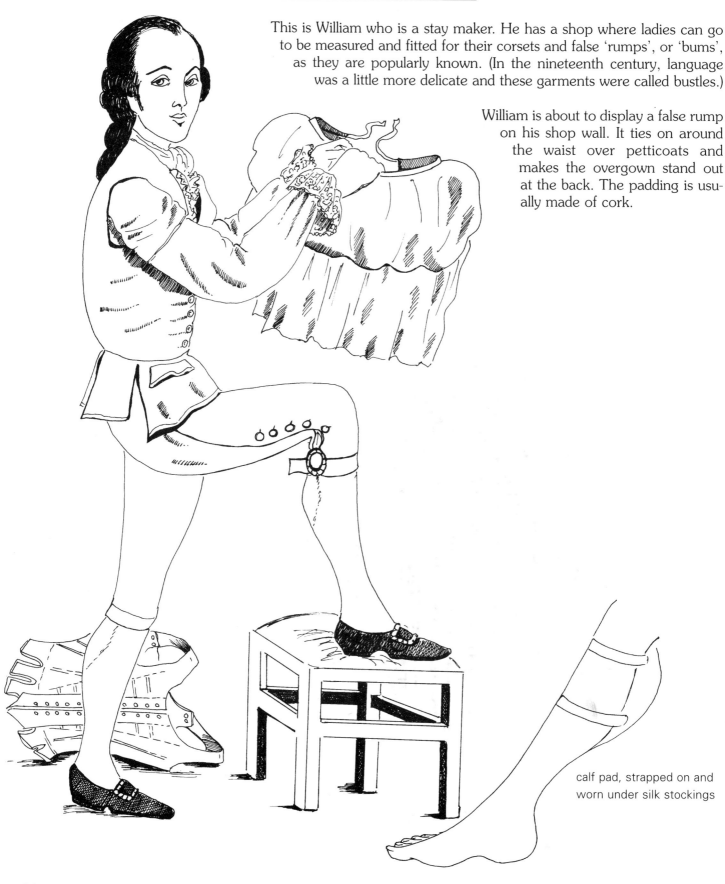

This is William who is a stay maker. He has a shop where ladies can go to be measured and fitted for their corsets and false 'rumps', or 'bums', as they are popularly known. (In the nineteenth century, language was a little more delicate and these garments were called bustles.)

William is about to display a false rump on his shop wall. It ties on around the waist over petticoats and makes the overgown stand out at the back. The padding is usually made of cork.

calf pad, strapped on and worn under silk stockings

Eleanor has come to William's shop to purchase a false rump to wear under her latest gown. The corset she is wearing is very heavily boned and has also been bought from William's shop. A similar corset is lying on the shop floor and you can see what it looks like from the back.

chemise

cork 'rump' or 'bum'

fawn cotton stays

It is not only women who squeeze themselves in and pad themselves out. It is fashionable for men to have muscular calves and as William has skinny legs, he is wearing false calves made from parchment under his white silk stockings! His shirt has a ruffle at the neck and extravagant lace cuffs and his breeches are very tight.

His breeches have detachable washable linings. Underneath these he is wearing short drawers fastened by a string around the waist.

petticoat

Fashion Revolution, 1800-1820

The French Revolution, with its cry of 'Freedom, Liberty and Equality', seemed to be mirrored by a similar revolution in fashion. The former rigid and structured styles disappeared and instead there was a vogue for slim, high-waisted dresses in diaphanous* materials that were worn with the minimum of underclothing.

This is Mary, the wife of a wealthy landowner. She is wearing a Classical-style dress in a light cotton fabric with only her chemise and one petticoat underneath.

As the waist is no longer accentuated, greater attention is given to the bust. Many women, including Mary's mother-in-law (seen on the opposite page), frequently wear false bosoms of wax or cotton or 'bust improvers' to enhance their natural shape.

Sometimes a small bustle is worn under the dress at the back. This could give the wearer a rather strange profile, referred to as the Grecian bend.

Women also began to wear drawers at this time. Decency made it essential for women to adopt this garment as the new light dresses were made of such flimsy material! Prior to this, drawers had been a purely masculine garment or were worn only by prostitutes, actresses and dancers and were therefore considered immodest. A pair of Mary's drawers are pictured opposite. They are made from cotton lawn. You can also see her maternity corset.

* diaphanous means fine and transparent

other speciality corsets of the time included one advertised to control the 'ills of excessive living' which promised to 'prevent flatulency and reduce protruberance'!

maternity corset, c. 1810

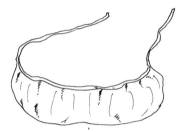

bustle stuffed with down

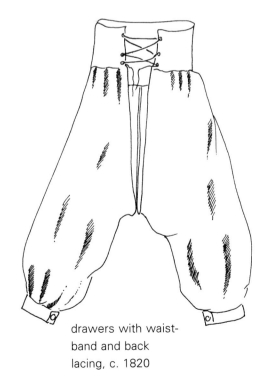

drawers with waist-band and back lacing, c. 1820

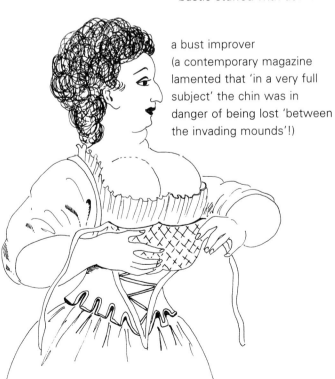

a bust improver
(a contemporary magazine lamented that 'in a very full subject' the chin was in danger of being lost 'between the invading mounds'!)

Pinched in and Puffed out, 1800-1820

This is Mary's brother John who is a dandy. This means that he spends a great deal of time and money on his appearance and is always immaculately dressed in the latest fashions.

His shirt collar is rigidly starched and has a frill down the front. He has a fashionably tiny waist which is achieved by wearing a tight corset and his chest is puffed out with the aid of a small cushion. He is wearing rouge and eau-de-cologne.

On the opposite page you can see John's friend Randolph, another dandy, who has his outerwear removed. Randolph is wearing a shirt, tightly-laced stays, breeches, calf pads and stockings. He is holding a quizzing glass which is the essential fashion accessory.

Being a dandy was often a painful business. There were reports that shirt collars and cravats were sometimes so stiff that ear lobes had been chopped off and throats cut. Some die-hards even went to the extreme of having their optic nerve loosened to make the use of a quizzing glass essential. All this goes to prove that it was not only women who were prepared to suffer for fashion!

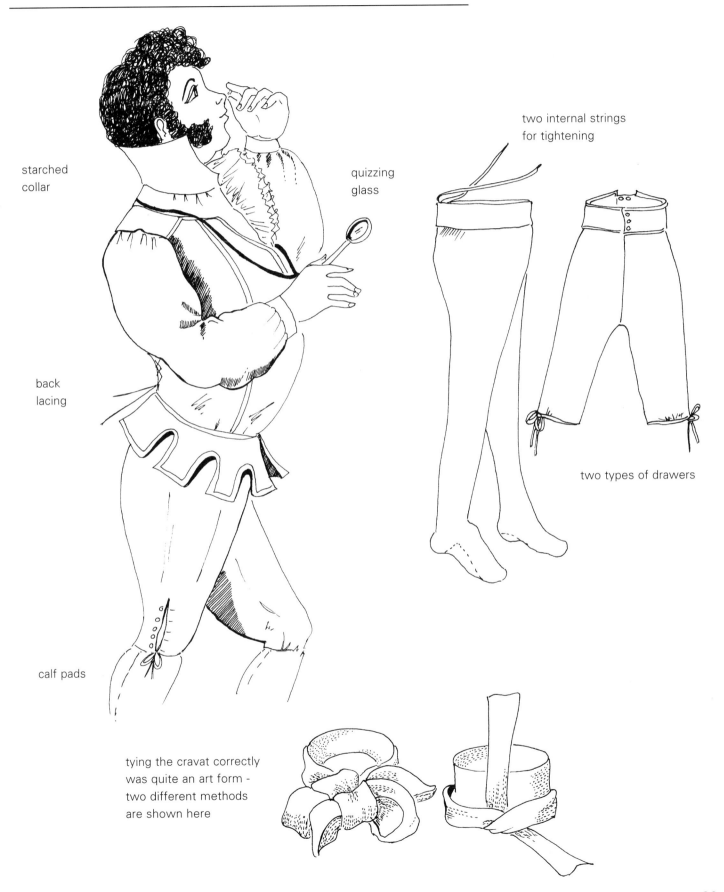

starched
collar

quizzing
glass

two internal strings
for tightening

back
lacing

two types of drawers

calf pads

tying the cravat correctly
was quite an art form -
two different methods
are shown here

The Return of the Waist, c. 1830

After the loose, classical styles of the early nineteenth century, the fashion pendulum swung again and women returned to wasp waists and tight lacing. Tiny waists were further accentuated by enormous puffed sleeves and billowing petticoats.

Constance is getting ready to go to a ball. She is wearing a boned corset over her chemise which is so tightly laced at the back that she will find it almost impossible to bend over. Her chemise's sleeves are padded and she is wearing several petticoats to hold out her skirts. The evening dress she will wear is pictured opposite.

Constance has several different corsets in her wardrobe. There is a special one for exercising and a demi-corset (only 20-24cm deep) which she wears for sleeping in. Metal eyelets have now been introduced and this means that it is possible to lace up the stays even tighter. With so much tight lacing and so many layers of petticoats, we can imagine that she must feel quite suffocated.

Constance's nightdress and nightcap are also shown opposite.

74cm

evening dress
with net over-
sleeves and
decorative apron

handmade
buttons

an exercise corset,
worn for archery

nightcap

Freedom from Petticoats, 1856

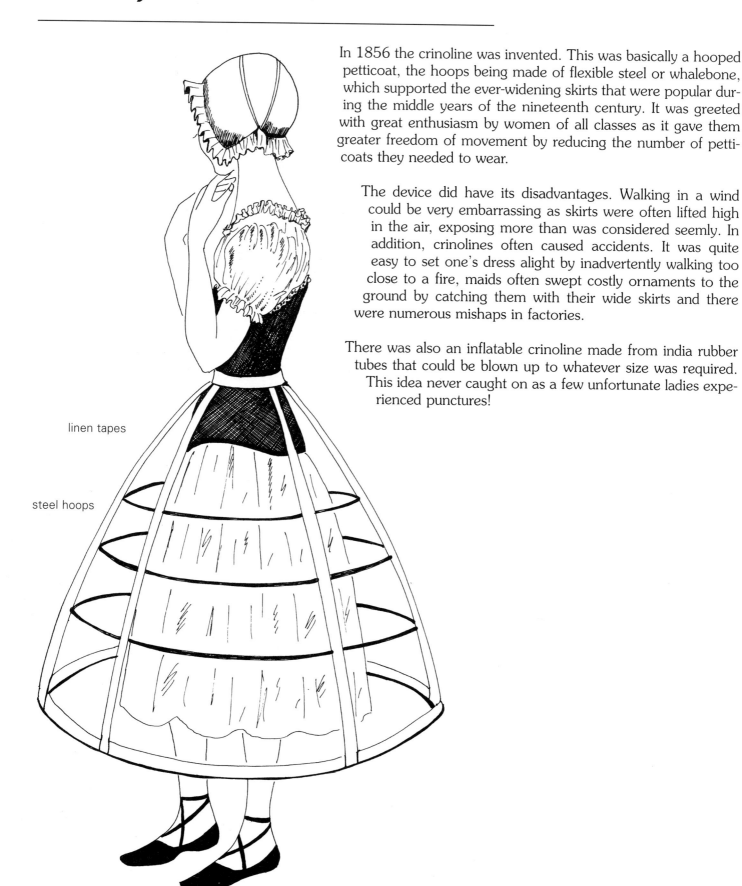

linen tapes

steel hoops

In 1856 the crinoline was invented. This was basically a hooped petticoat, the hoops being made of flexible steel or whalebone, which supported the ever-widening skirts that were popular during the middle years of the nineteenth century. It was greeted with great enthusiasm by women of all classes as it gave them greater freedom of movement by reducing the number of petticoats they needed to wear.

The device did have its disadvantages. Walking in a wind could be very embarrassing as skirts were often lifted high in the air, exposing more than was considered seemly. In addition, crinolines often caused accidents. It was quite easy to set one's dress alight by inadvertently walking too close to a fire, maids often swept costly ornaments to the ground by catching them with their wide skirts and there were numerous mishaps in factories.

There was also an inflatable crinoline made from india rubber tubes that could be blown up to whatever size was required. This idea never caught on as a few unfortunate ladies experienced punctures!

The codpiece and tights from the fifteenth century reappear in the Jean-Paul Gaultier design of 1990.

c. 1990

early fifteenth century

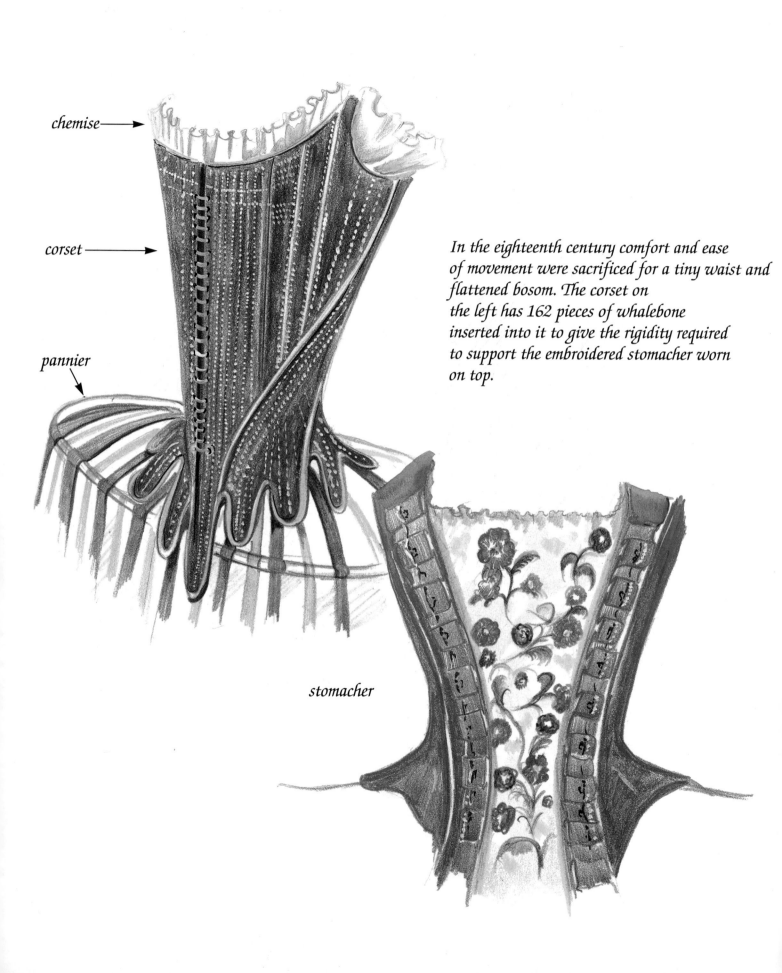

chemise

corset

pannier

stomacher

In the eighteenth century comfort and ease of movement were sacrificed for a tiny waist and flattened bosom. The corset on the left has 162 pieces of whalebone inserted into it to give the rigidity required to support the embroidered stomacher worn on top.

Until recent times children of wealthy families dressed as miniature adults and therefore wore the same underwear. The girl from 1740 is wearing a rigid bodice and layers of petticoats. Two centuries later, young girls were still wearing corsets and shoulder braces like the one shown here.

c. 1900

c. 1740

Being a fashionable dandy was a painful business and required assistance. The high starched collar, tight corset and calf pads must have been extremely uncomfortable. The gentleman on the left has strategically placed cushions to give him a puffed out chest and more muscular arms.

c. 1819

The long slim line of 1913 was not achieved without restricting underwear...

c. 1913

The flattened flapper with her slim hips and short skirt
wears a long-line corset to achieve her boyish look.

c. 1920

Fashionable nightwear c. 1986

Eighteenth-century bodice decorated with flowers and stiffened with rush.

This evening gown of 1994 has a rigid, boned bodice that requires no underwear and is reminiscent of the bodices worn in the eighteenth century.

Padding out the Behind, 1870-1888

During the 1870s and 1880s it was fashionable for all the fullness of a lady's skirt to be at the back. Women wore bustles in various shapes and sizes to achieve this style. Sometimes the bustle was a pad stuffed with cotton wool or feathers that would be tied on around the waist or it could form part of a petticoat or even be a separate cage-like structure.

Once again, being fashionable could have its disadvantages. Serving girls who could not afford the real thing often stuffed dusters or newspapers up their skirts instead. These could fall out unexpectedly or move out of position. There is even a story of a lady who, when out walking in Chester, was set upon by a donkey because her bustle was stuffed with bran!

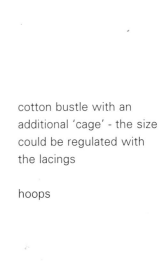

cotton bustle with an additional 'cage' - the size could be regulated with the lacings

hoops

Victorian Secrets, 1860-1890

Lord Thomas and his wife Emma live with their family and servants on a large estate in Hampshire. They dress in the latest fashions and always look charming but underneath they are often very uncomfortable. They both wear tight-fitting corsets and Emma occasionally wears an additional 'stoop cure' in order to keep an upright posture as no lady 'should be able to see her buttons'.*

On these two pages you can see items of underwear from their wardrobes. Can you find out any more Victorian secrets?

undershirt

* *Home Notes* July 1894

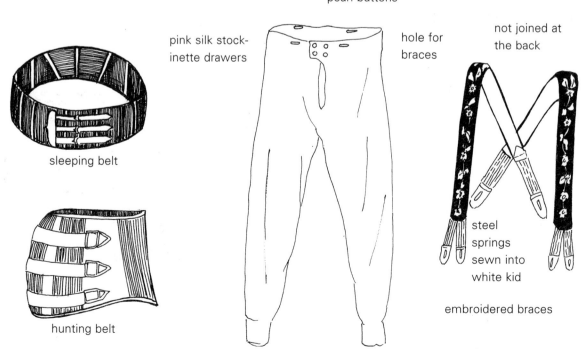

sleeping belt

hunting belt

pink silk stock-
inette drawers

pearl buttons

hole for
braces

not joined at
the back

steel
springs
sewn into
white kid

embroidered braces

long-line corset,
1880

a support belt
to 'restore
'shapeliness',
1894

a 'stoop cure' for
round shoulders and
weak backs

c. 1884

bust improvers
worn under the camisole

c. 1890

different size pads could be
worn with these

drawers elaborately
trimmed with lace,
1860-70

suspenders
on a sateen
band, 1881 -
invented
1876

The Reform Movement

c. 1884

During the late nineteenth and early twentieth centuries a 'Reform Movement' in dress occurred. This was a reaction against the harmful effects of fashion. It was supported by some artists and literary people who felt that only what was natural could be beautiful and that tightly-laced corsets and cumbersome bustles should be discarded. Instead, they advocated corsets that gently supported rather than constricted the body and dresses with soft flowing lines.

Dr Gustav Jaeger was an influential figure at this time. He had a theory that only animal fibres could prevent the retention of the 'noxious exhalations' of the body and claimed that only wool should be worn next to the skin. He introduced his 'sanitory system' of woollen underwear in the 1880s. He also believed that it was better for men to wear breeches rather than trousers as breeches stopped harmful draughts going up the legs! Oscar Wilde and George Bernard Shaw were two devotees of the Jaeger system.

Aertex was another innovation of the early 1900s. This was a fabric that was full of holes and the idea was that the holes trapped air which kept you warm in winter and cool in summer.

Harriet is an artist and feminist and believes passionately that women should be comfortable in their clothes. She is wearing a dress of brocaded silk with puff sleeves and a flowing skirt. Underneath, she has on a reform corset, a chemise, one petticoat and knitted drawers. Perhaps you could compare her dress and underwear with fashions for 1884.

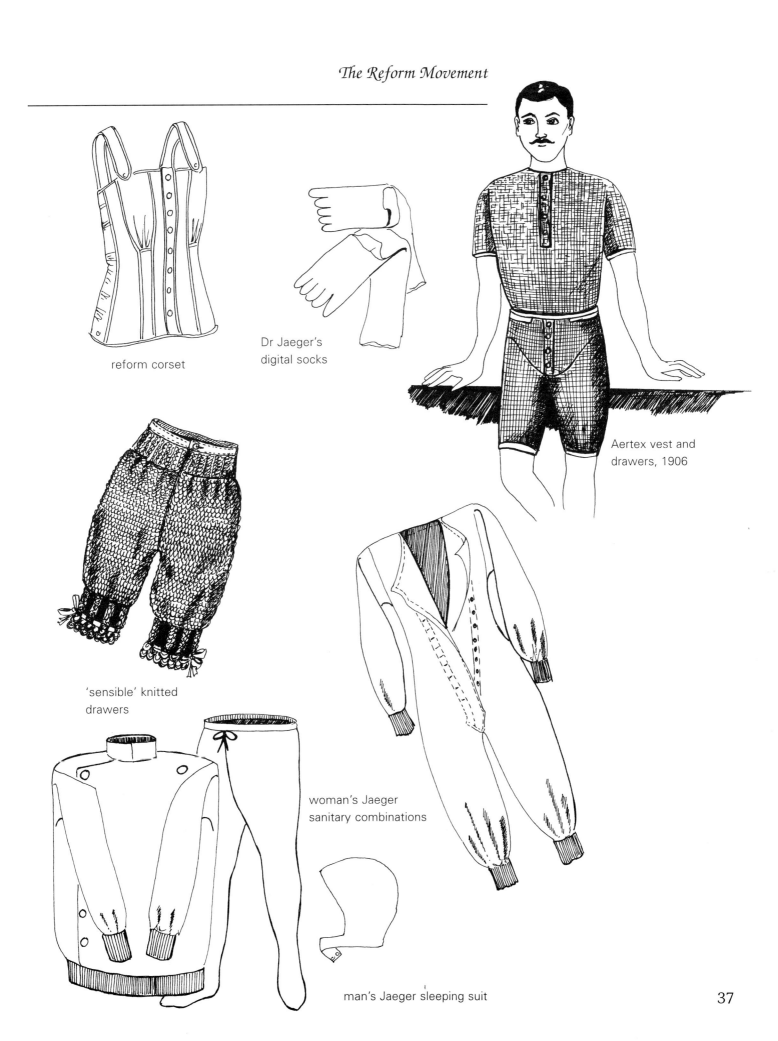

reform corset

Dr Jaeger's digital socks

Aertex vest and drawers, 1906

'sensible' knitted drawers

woman's Jaeger sanitary combinations

man's Jaeger sleeping suit

Frou-frou* and Lace, c. 1905

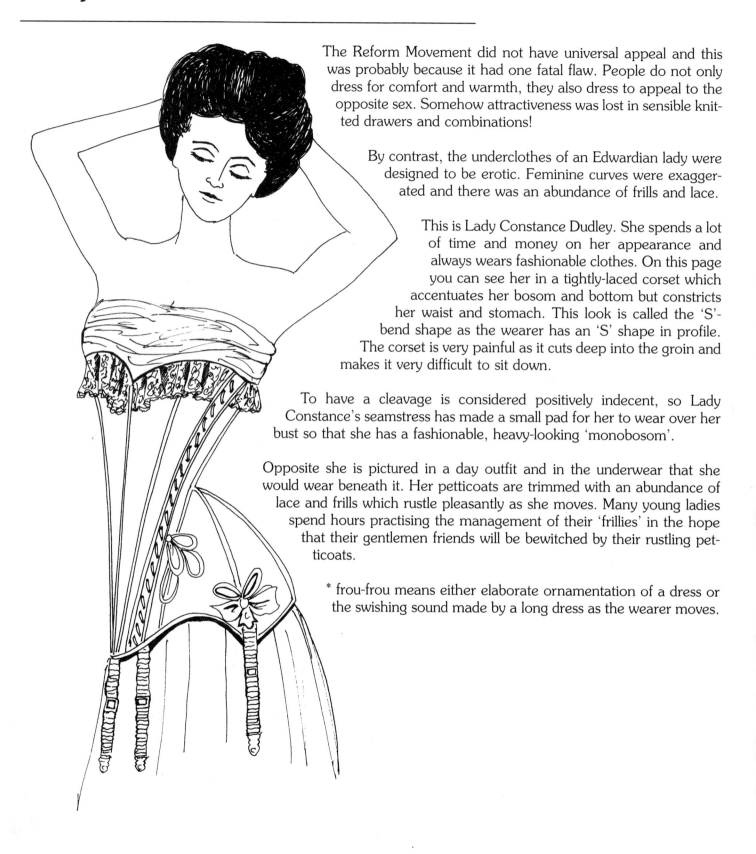

The Reform Movement did not have universal appeal and this was probably because it had one fatal flaw. People do not only dress for comfort and warmth, they also dress to appeal to the opposite sex. Somehow attractiveness was lost in sensible knitted drawers and combinations!

By contrast, the underclothes of an Edwardian lady were designed to be erotic. Feminine curves were exaggerated and there was an abundance of frills and lace.

This is Lady Constance Dudley. She spends a lot of time and money on her appearance and always wears fashionable clothes. On this page you can see her in a tightly-laced corset which accentuates her bosom and bottom but constricts her waist and stomach. This look is called the 'S'-bend shape as the wearer has an 'S' shape in profile. The corset is very painful as it cuts deep into the groin and makes it very difficult to sit down.

To have a cleavage is considered positively indecent, so Lady Constance's seamstress has made a small pad for her to wear over her bust so that she has a fashionable, heavy-looking 'monobosom'.

Opposite she is pictured in a day outfit and in the underwear that she would wear beneath it. Her petticoats are trimmed with an abundance of lace and frills which rustle pleasantly as she moves. Many young ladies spend hours practising the management of their 'frillies' in the hope that their gentlemen friends will be bewitched by their rustling petticoats.

* frou-frou means either elaborate ornamentation of a dress or the swishing sound made by a long dress as the wearer moves.

waist petticoat and
camisole, c. 1906

knickers with a side
fastening are beginning
to replace drawers as
they give a smoother
line over the hips

Hobble and Tango, 1908-1914

The 'S'-bend shape and extravagantly frilly petti-coats began to disappear around 1907 and were replaced by a slimmer look. This was partly due to the influence of the French couturier Paul Poiret who introduced a straight up-and-down line. Corsets became nearly tubular in shape and were very long, sometimes measuring up to 60cm down the back. Poiret also introduced the hobble skirt which was so tight around the ankles that the wearer was forced to walk with short, mincing steps.

the tango craze

Elizabeth is a debutante who loves to wear the latest fashions. On the opposite page she is dressed in a hobble skirt and you can also see some of the formidable underwear she might wear underneath it. These fashions are not practical for one of Elizabeth's favourite pastimes - dancing the tango! For this her skirt is draped or slit up the front, revealing her tango shoes.

Elizabeth has a friend in America who has sent her one of the first brassières to try. It has been designed by Caresse Crosby, an American debutante, and is revolutionary in that for the first time the breasts are separated. Caresse thought up the idea using two handkerchiefs and ribbon!

1913

long-line corset,
1909

Caresse Crosby's
brassière design,
1914

1912

hobble
petticoat with
removable
steel hoops

Slim Lines and Flatteners, 1920-1939

c. 1925

The emancipation of women after the First World War had a profound effect on fashion. As women were now 'equal' to men, fashion seemed to want to emphasize this by suppressing their feminine characteristics. Busts were flattened, hips were slimmed, waists were by-passed, hair was cropped and the ideal figure was a straight line. By the 1930s, this boyish look had given way to a more elegant line but the emphasis was still on slimness. A greater variety of underwear was available and advances in technology, leading to the increased use of elastic and the introduction of the zip fastener, meant that it was more comfortable to wear.

Emmeline is the daughter of a wealthy Colonel. She leads a hectic social life and loves to go out dancing with her friends at night. She is wearing a reducing corset over her chemise and silk stockings. The new short skirts have created a demand for flesh-coloured stockings to flatter newly-exposed legs but the first nylon stockings will not appear until 1938 in America.

On the next page, you can see Emmeline in a flattener bra and an elastic corset. Her friend Gloria is wearing long camiknickers. These look like a petticoat but have a divided skirt and a gusset under the crotch. On the far right, Emmeline is pictured in the kind of underwear she will wear in the next decade.

During the 1930s sizing was introduced for lady's underwear. It was also at this time that the brassière came to be called simply the 'bra' and underwear referred to as 'undies'.

1920-1939

printed camiknickers trimmed with ribbon bows, c. 1921

satin brassière and new silk elastic pull-on belt, c. 1923

lace bra and silk girdle with elastic inserts, c. 1935

crochet bra, c. 1931

knitted backless evening dress vest, c. 1931

drawers, c. 1927

Air Cooled and Striped, c. 1935

Men's underwear changed very little during the first part of the twentieth century. By the 1930s, however, some new and more colourful styles were beginning to emerge that had originated in America.

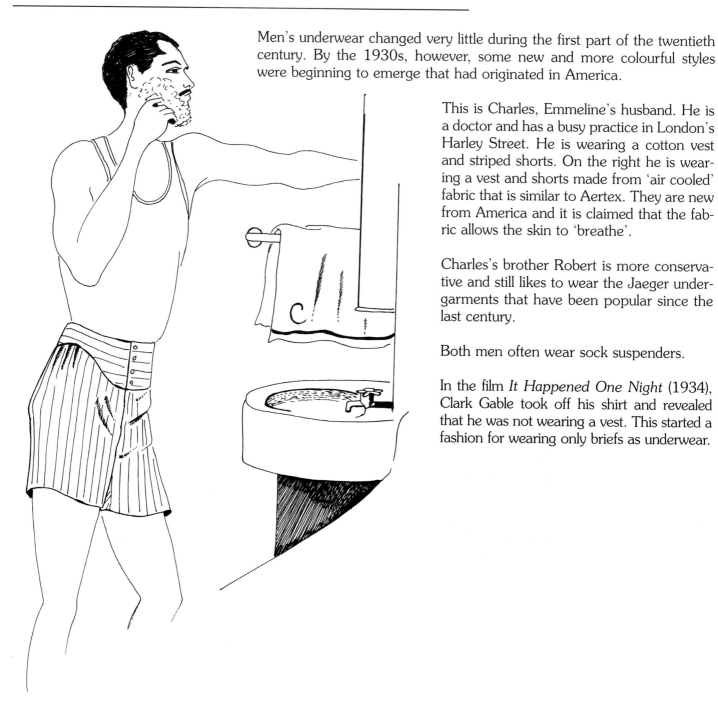

This is Charles, Emmeline's husband. He is a doctor and has a busy practice in London's Harley Street. He is wearing a cotton vest and striped shorts. On the right he is wearing a vest and shorts made from 'air cooled' fabric that is similar to Aertex. They are new from America and it is claimed that the fabric allows the skin to 'breathe'.

Charles's brother Robert is more conservative and still likes to wear the Jaeger undergarments that have been popular since the last century.

Both men often wear sock suspenders.

In the film *It Happened One Night* (1934), Clark Gable took off his shirt and revealed that he was not wearing a vest. This started a fashion for wearing only briefs as underwear.

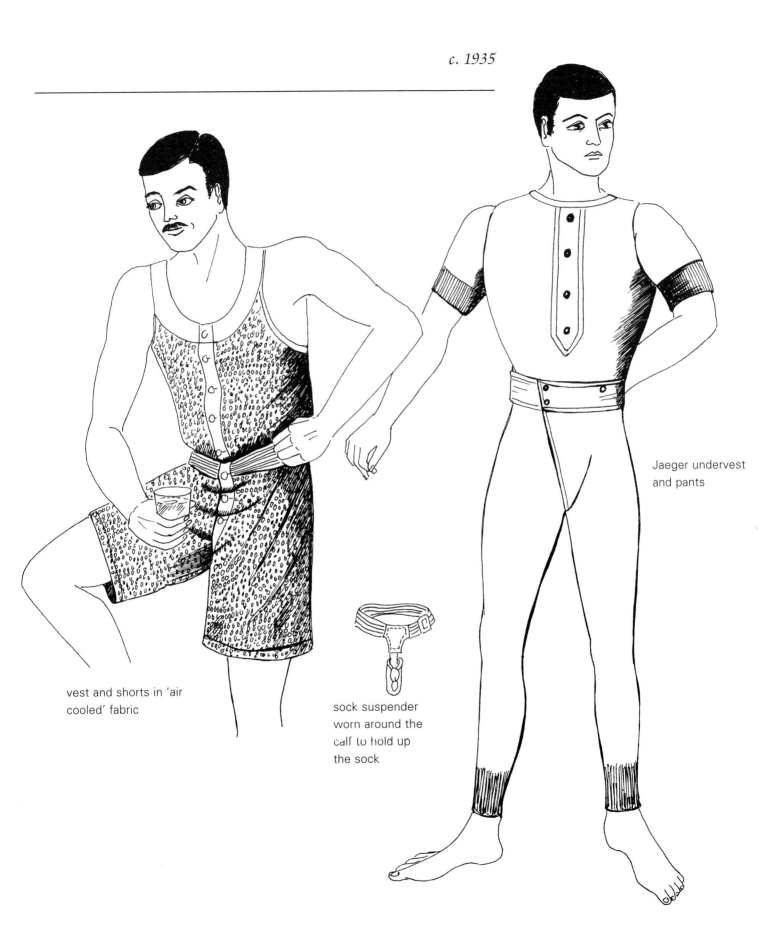

vest and shorts in 'air
cooled' fabric

sock suspender
worn around the
calf to hold up
the sock

Jaeger undervest
and pants

Wartime Ingenuity, c. 1943

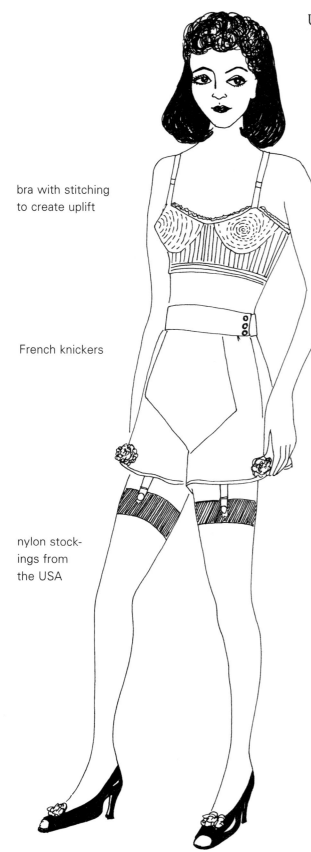

bra with stitching
to create uplift

French knickers

nylon stock-
ings from
the USA

Underwear, like all clothing, was subject to rationing during the Second World War and the undergarments produced through the Utility Scheme (which restricted the amount of material that could be used for clothes) were more practical than pretty. This meant that women used their ingenuity to create their own garments and glamour.

Knitting was a favourite blackout occupation and some women knitted underwear for themselves. Others used their needlework skills to turn old curtains and dresses into fancy petticoats and knickers. Sometimes, worn parachutes were released to civilians and the material from these was often turned into lingerie. Stockings were hard to come by and many girls resorted to painting fake ones on to their legs and then drawing in a seam with eye pencil. Women working in the forces had to be content with service issue clothes. The rayon knickers in drab colours they had to wear were considered so unflattering that they had nicknames like 'passion killers' and 'boy bafflers'.

Joan is working for the WLA (Women's Land Army) on a farm in the country and she is pictured here in her underwear. She is the envy of her friends because her American boyfriend has brought her some nylon stockings from the USA.

The farm where Joan is stationed is owned by Fred and Edith Westlake. They have several evacuees and visitors staying with them and Edith's washing line often looks a real picture when she has hung out all the different kinds of underwear!

Men's undergarments changed very little at this time. Some of Edith's son's underwear is hanging on her line.

rayon 'passion killers'

French knickers made from curtain material

knitted knickers

petticoat made from parachute material

jockey trunks

vest

Uplift and Waspies, c. 1948

When Christian Dior launched his New Look designs in 1947 they were seized upon by fashion-starved women who were tired of the drabness of the war years. Women longed to be feminine again and emphasized their curves by squeezing in their waists, uplifting their breasts and padding their tops, and the new full skirts were supported by billowing petticoats. Glamorous Hollywood film stars like Jane Russell and Lana Turner helped to promote the fashion for an hourglass figure and thousands of women tried to copy their looks.

Audrey Somerville is a lawyer's wife. She loves the feminine fashions and is seen here in a New Look petticoat and matching corselette. It is fashionable to have a very tiny waist so she frequently squeezes herself in to a 'Waspie' corset which is laced up very tightly at the back. Can you compare these fashions with another time in history when it was desirable to have a 'wasp' waist?

Once again, there was little change in men's underwear at this time, except that in 1946 Jockey patented the Y-front construction for men's underpants. They were advertised as having been 'scientifically perfected for correct masculine support'!

satin 'Waspie' girdle
with padded hips and
back lacing, 1947

boned and back-laced
'Waspie' corset in
nylon and satin,
c. 1948

nylon bra with elastic
insert in front, 1948

men's Y-fronts, 1946

Jane Russell in the film
The Outlaw (1943).
An uplift bra was required
to achieve this high
profile! The film was
banned for six years
because it was thought
immoral.

Padding and Petticoats, The 1950s

Underwear was transformed in the 1950s by the increased use of nylon. Lightweight, hardwearing garments that could be easily cared for were available on the mass market which meant that all classes could now afford them. Advertising laws were relaxed in the middle of the decade and underwear was advertised on television for the first time. This had a powerful influence in promoting new styles. Bosoms were 'in' and there were falsies, padded bras and even 'inflatable' bras to give uplift to those who felt they needed it. The most popular bra of the decade was the 'sweater girl' bra which provided an exaggerated high bosom by means of padding and stitching.

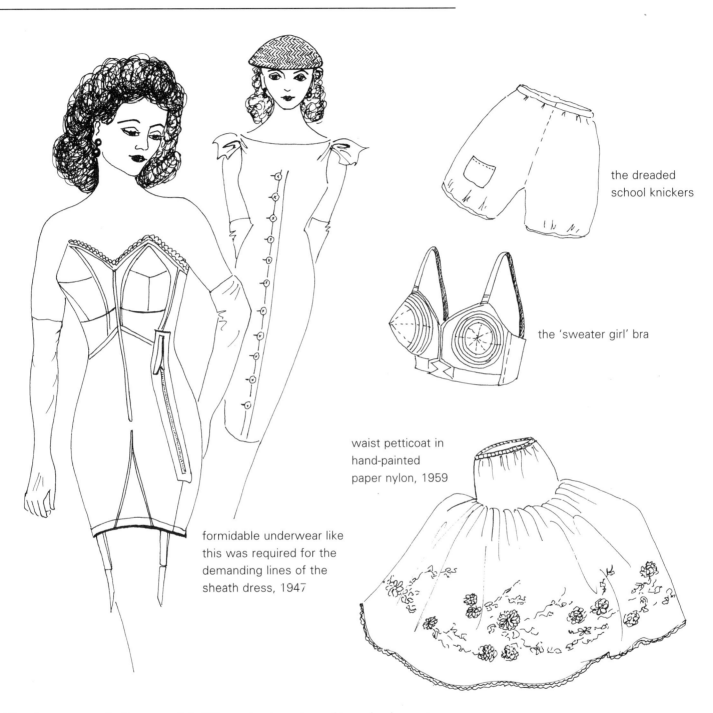

the dreaded
school knickers

the 'sweater girl' bra

waist petticoat in
hand-painted
paper nylon, 1959

formidable underwear like
this was required for the
demanding lines of the
sheath dress, 1947

Alice is a young fashion model. When she is not working she loves to go
to the Mecca with her boyfriend where they dance the rock 'n' roll. She
is wearing a strapless, padded and boned long-line bra and a petticoat
made from 50 yards (c. 46m) of nylon which she will wear under her new
dirndl skirt. Alice's sister Susan prefers the fashionable 'sheath' dress
which shows *every* curve of her body, so requiring controlling underwear
underneath it! Both girls often laugh about the horrors of the cotton,
fleecy-lined school knickers that they used to have to wear. They were hot
and itchy and came in dull colours like navy, bottle green, grey and brown.

Young Fashion, The 1960s

The 1960s were an exciting time in the fashion world. For the first time in history, young people set the trends with new and outrageous designs that shocked the older generation. The mini skirt dominated the decade and was remarkable in that it exposed the female leg up to and including the thighs. This meant that stockings and suspenders were no longer acceptable and tights became fashionable. Feminists urged women to 'burn their bras' and young girls wore the minimum of underclothing under the simple 'A' line fashions. There was a brief vogue for topless dresses around 1965 and the 'no-bra bra' which was transparent and designed to be worn by those who did not really need one! Lycra (invented in 1959) enabled manufacturers to produce sleek, figure-hugging underwear, and co-ordinated underwear sets were also available in printed tricot (a rayon or nylon fabric resembling knitting).

Nicola owns her own boutique where she sells fashionable clothes to young people at affordable prices. On the left she is wearing red and white striped underwear with matching socks. These have been designed by Mary Quant. On the right you can see some examples of items from her shop. She sells quite a few panty-girdles with outrageous designs on them, proving, perhaps, that even in the free and easy 1960s many women still like to feel that their figures are being controlled!

1965

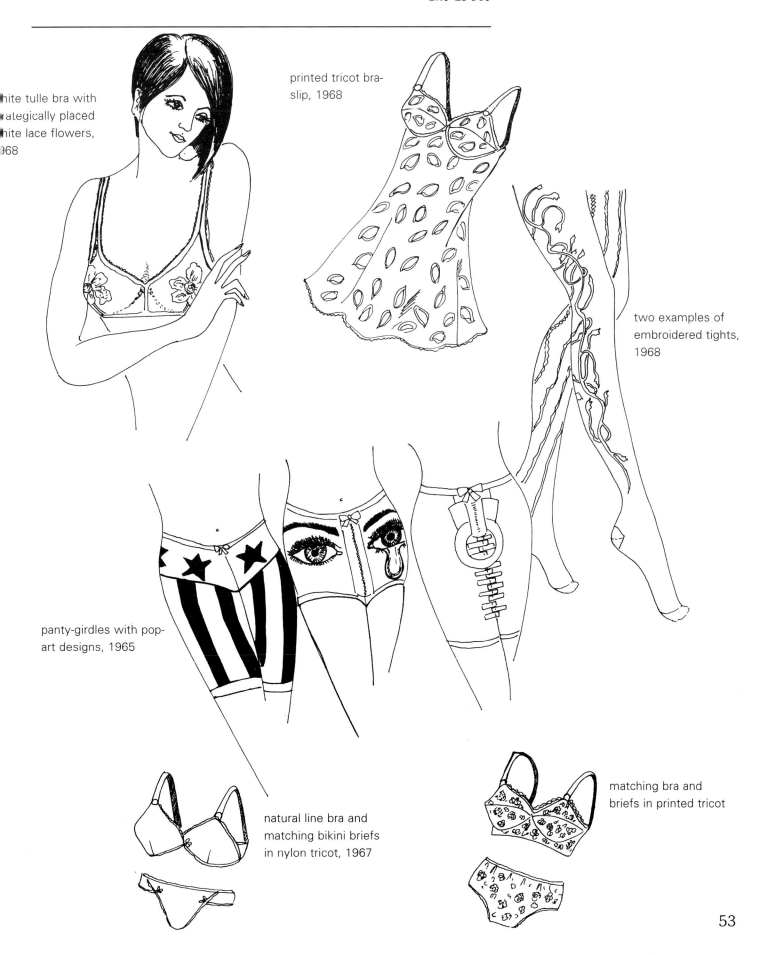

white tulle bra with strategically placed white lace flowers, 1968

printed tricot bra-slip, 1968

two examples of embroidered tights, 1968

panty-girdles with pop-art designs, 1965

natural line bra and matching bikini briefs in nylon tricot, 1967

matching bra and briefs in printed tricot

Young Fashion, Old Fashioned, The 1960s

plain coloured vest and Y-fronts
and brief, patterned, clingy
pants, c. 1969

Since Victorian times men's clothes had been rather conventional and dull, but suddenly, in the 1960s, menswear received an injection of colour and style. This was largely due to the influence of young dynamic designers like John Stephens who opened boutiques in Carnaby Street selling colourful and original men's garments. These changes are sometimes referred to as the peacock revolution.

Nicola's boyfriend Robert likes to wear the latest fashions. His shirt, with its neck and wrist frills and elaborate bow, is reminiscent both of Elizabethan and Regency styles. As the shirt is now worn more often without a waistcoat, it could be regarded more as outer rather than underwear.

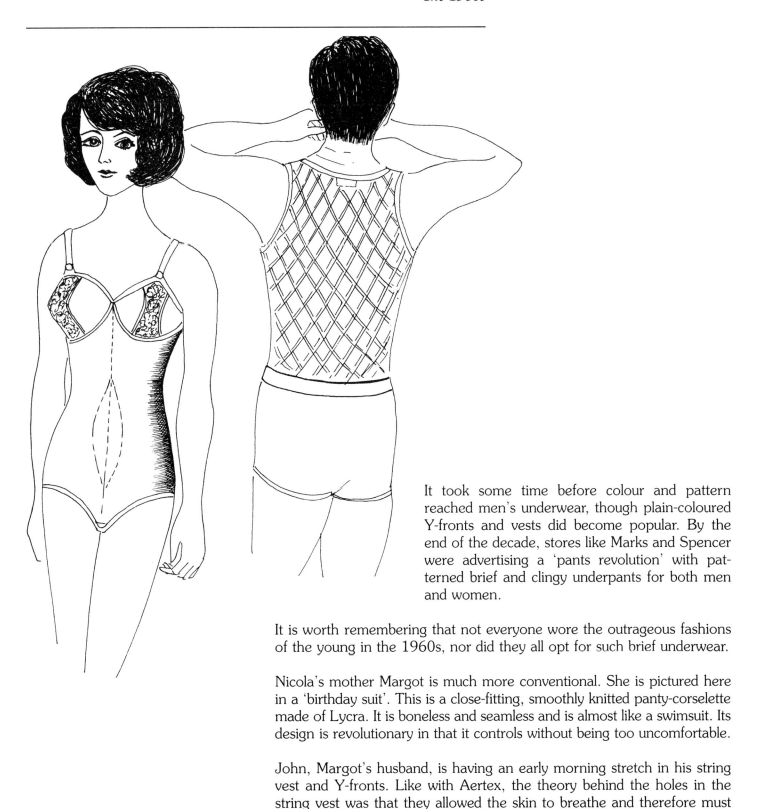

It took some time before colour and pattern reached men's underwear, though plain-coloured Y-fronts and vests did become popular. By the end of the decade, stores like Marks and Spencer were advertising a 'pants revolution' with patterned brief and clingy underpants for both men and women.

It is worth remembering that not everyone wore the outrageous fashions of the young in the 1960s, nor did they all opt for such brief underwear.

Nicola's mother Margot is much more conventional. She is pictured here in a 'birthday suit'. This is a close-fitting, smoothly knitted panty-corselette made of Lycra. It is boneless and seamless and is almost like a swimsuit. Its design is revolutionary in that it controls without being too uncomfortable.

John, Margot's husband, is having an early morning stretch in his string vest and Y-fronts. Like with Aertex, the theory behind the holes in the string vest was that they allowed the skin to breathe and therefore must be healthy.

Feminism versus Femininity, The 1970s

There was a sense of confusion in the fashion world during the 1970s. Hemlines went up and down with mini and maxi skirts, and hot pants and flared trousers could be seen on the street together. These contradictions appeared to be reflected in underwear styles. Feminists were still arguing for a ban on the bra, while figure-hugging jersey dresses and skin-tight jeans demanded underwear that was ultra smooth. At the same time, however, glamorous undergarments were popular, a good example being the Wonderbra. This was made from 26 separate parts and with its plunging neckline and padded cups was guaranteed to provide an impressive cleavage. The Wonderbra went on to become the top-selling bra in the world, and is enjoying renewed popularity in the 1990s.

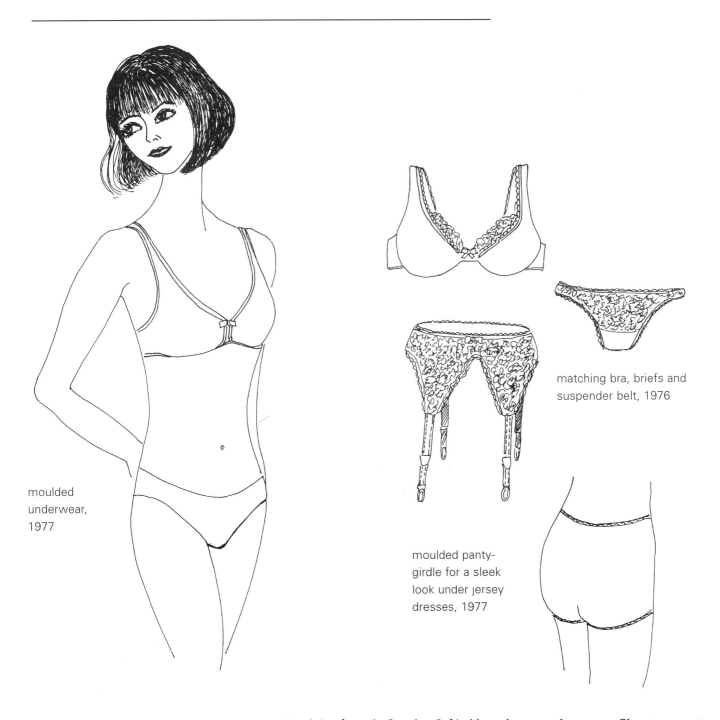

moulded underwear, 1977

matching bra, briefs and suspender belt, 1976

moulded panty-girdle for a sleek look under jersey dresses, 1977

Nicola's friend Sandy (left) likes lace underwear. She is wearing a Wonderbra and a lacy half slip designed by Janet Reger. Sandy owns several lacy bra and brief sets and also likes to wear stockings and suspenders which have come back into fashion.

Nicola, on the other hand, prefers smooth, invisible undergarments and likes moulded underwear. This is when garments have been produced from a single piece of material which is then moulded into shape. She also prefers tights to stockings and sometimes wears tights that have built-in panties or body shapers.

Fitness and Glamour, The 1980s

c. 1988

The health and fitness boom of the 1980s had a considerable effect on underclothing. Designs frequently reflected the influence of sportswear, with boxer shorts, cropped tops, sports bras and leggings becoming popular. Both men and women demanded clothes that fitted like a second skin in order to show off their newly-sculptured bodies and lycra provided this look.

In contrast to this, there was a revival in glamorous lacy and boned corsets and long-line bras. These were more decorative than tortuous and were worn by a generation of women who had never known constricting underwear and who regarded the corset as an item of glamour rather than pain.

Gabrielle and Geoff are a young professional couple who earn large salaries and have a multi-activity lifestyle. Gabrielle is wearing a boned basque* with matching briefs and a co-ordinating silk wrap. Geoff has been at the gym and is displaying his muscular body in a lycra vest and matching briefs, both of which are rather more decorative than practical!

Other items from their wardrobe are pictured opposite. Can you see any resemblance between some of these designs and underwear from previous centuries?

* basque is a late twentieth-century term for corset

the invisible corset of diet
and exercise worn with
minimal underwear

c. 1989

sports bra, 1989

cotton cropped
top and matching
briefs, 1989

men's boxer
shorts and mini
briefs, 1986-90

Conclusion, The 1990s

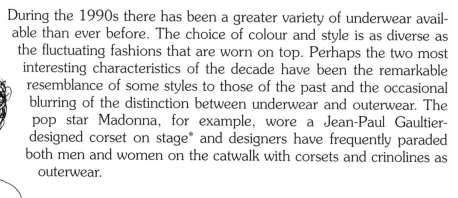

During the 1990s there has been a greater variety of underwear available than ever before. The choice of colour and style is as diverse as the fluctuating fashions that are worn on top. Perhaps the two most interesting characteristics of the decade have been the remarkable resemblance of some styles to those of the past and the occasional blurring of the distinction between underwear and outerwear. The pop star Madonna, for example, wore a Jean-Paul Gaultier-designed corset on stage* and designers have frequently paraded both men and women on the catwalk with corsets and crinolines as outerwear.

Here Gabrielle is wearing a dress with a laced bodice without undergarments which is very similar to the medieval gown on page 10. Geoff is wearing a cotton and polyester bodysuit which is really rather like Victorian combinations!

More 1990s underwear is pictured on the next page.

It seems that men and women will continue to strive to alter their natural body shape by artificial means in order to be fashionable. Why do you think this is? What do you think the next fashionable 'shape' will be?

* you can see this outfit on page 64

black lacy
basque, boned
and under-
wired, 1991

white cotton corset with
lace sleeves and white
cotton leggings, 1990

strapless under-
wired bra, 1991

men's boxer shorts and briefs in
bright colours, 1994

men's and women's tanga
briefs, 1994

bodysuit, 1994

Glossary and Selected Index

Quant, Mary	*(page 52)*
quizzing glass	a small monocle *(page 29)*
Reger, Janet	*(page 56)*
ruff	a circular, pleated and gathered piece of material worn at the neck and wrists *(pages 14, 15, 17)*
'S'-bend corset	a corset designed to crush the stomach and cut into the groin, so giving the wearer an 'S' shape in profile *(page 38)*
shirt	man's undergarment *(pages 8, 13, 18, 19, 24, 28, 29, 54)*
slashes	cuts made into material for decoration *(pages 12, 18)*
smock	the Saxon name for chemise *(page 9)*
sports bra	a bra designed as sportswear *(page 59)*
stockings	woven or knitted covering for the legs *(pages 18, 19, 21, 29, 46)*
stoop cure	a device worn to correct the posture *(page 35)*
stomacher	an ornamental panel made of rich and embroidered material and inserted in the front of a doublet or gown *(page 15)*
support belt	a girdle worn by men *(page 35)*
suspender belt	an elastic strap with a fastener at the end worn to hold up stockings or socks *(pages 35, 38, 41, 42, 43, 45, 46, 49, 51, 55, 57, 61)*
sweater girl bra	a bra designed to give an exaggerated high bosom *(page 51)*
tanga	brief pants made from two triangles of material and joined at the hips by thin strips of material *(pages 59, 61)*
tights	one piece covering for the feet and legs which reaches the waist *(page 53)*
tricot	thin rayon or nylon material that is knitted or resembles knitting *(page 53)*
tulle	fine net fabric of silk or rayon *(page 52)*
vest	a sleeveless garment worn by men and women for warmth *(pages 44, 45, 47, 54, 55)*
waspie	a term applied to corsets designed to create a tiny waist in the 1940s and 1950s *(page 48)*
Wonderbra	an underwired and padded bra designed to display the breasts *(page 56)*
Y-fronts	men's underpants with a Y-shaped fly *(pages 49, 54)*

Book list

Anderson, Black J. and Garland, M.	*A history of fashion*, Orbis, 2nd ed., 1980
Angeloglou, M.	*A history of make-up*, Studio Vista, 1970
Ash, Juliet and Wilson, Elizabeth (eds.)	*Chic thrills*, Harper Collins, 1992
Bailey, Adrian	*The passion for fashion*, Dragon's World, 1988
Bell, Quentin	*On human finery*, Hogarth Press, 1976
Bond, David	*Guinness guide to 20th century fashion*, 1988
Bradfield, Nancy	*Costume in detail 1730-1930*, Harrap, 1968
Canter Cremers van der Does, Eline	*The agony of fashion*, Blandford Press, 1980
Carter, Alison	*Underwear, the fashion history*, Batsford, 1992
Cohn, Nik	*Today there are no gentlemen*, Weidenfeld and Nicolson, 1971
Cunnington, C. Willet and Phillis	*The history of underclothes*, Faber and Faber, revised ed., 1981
De Marly, Diana	*Fashion for men*, Batsford, 1985
Ewing, Elizabeth	*Dress and undress*, Batsford, 1979
Ewing, Elizabeth	*Fashion in underwear*, Batsford
Farrell, Jeremy	*Socks and sockings*, Batsford, 1992
Foster, V.	*A visual history of costume in the 19th century*, Batsford, 1984
Glynn, Prudence	*In fashion - dress in the 20th century*, George Allen & Unwin, 1978
Grass, Milton E.	*History of hosiery*, Fairchild Pulications, 1953
Hall, C.A.	*From hoopskirts to nudity:*
	A review of the follies and foibles of fashion 1866-1936, Caldwell, 1938
Lurie, Alison	*The language of clothes*, Heinemann, 1981
McDowell, Colin	*Dressed to kill - sex and power in clothes*, Hutchinson, 1992
Peacock, John	*20th century fashion*, Thames & Hudson, 1993
Ribiero, Aileen	*Dress and morality*, Batsford, 1980
Saint-Laurent, Cecil	*A history of ladies' underwear*, Michael Joseph, 1968
St Michael, Mick	*Madonna in her own words*, Omnibus Press, 1990
Steele, Valerie	*Fashion and eroticism*, OUP, 1985
Waugh, Norah	*Corsets and crinolines*, Batsford, 2nd imp., 1970
White, Cynthia, L.	*Women's magazines 1693-1968*, Michael Joseph, 1970

Things to Do

1 Throughout the centuries men and women have worn constricting underwear in order to try and alter their natural shape. This has often had a harmful effect on their health. Investigate some of the ways in which underwear has caused physical damage.

2 In the past, ideas about cleanliness were very different to those of today. Some women, for example, wore their corsets until they rotted without ever washing them. Find out more about keeping clean and, in particular, about caring for and washing undergarments.

3 Compare the effect of the French Revolution on fashion and underwear with that of the youth revolution of the 1960s.

4 Do a project on the history of stockings.

5 Look at revivals in fashionable underwear. See how many styles you can find reappearing from the past.

6 Ideas about modesty are different now to how they used to be. For example, in ancient times women frequently wore no covering for the breasts and in the eighteenth century it was customary for a lady to entertain visitors in her bedroom while she was getting dressed. Investigate changing ideas of modesty. Are we more or less prudish than in the past?

7 In former times children of wealthy families always wore the same constricting undergarments as their parents. Find out what they wore in a period of your choice. What might the harmful effects be?

c. 1990